DATE DUE

JAN 1 4 1978			
JUN 1 1978	SEP 19 1995		
JUL 2 2 1981	JUN 3 1998		
MAR 1 0 1983	APR 2 1999		
SEP 9 1985	JUN 18 2001		
MAY 1 5 1986	JUN 28 '01		
JUL 1 0 1986			
MAY 28 1987			
MAR 2 6 1990			
APR 2 6 1990			
JAN 2 7 1993			
JUN 2 9 1993			
MAY 1 6 1995			
AUG 1 1995			

weird
gardens

Cameron and Margaret Yerian, Editors

 CHILDRENS PRESS, CHICAGO

Executive Editors
Cameron John Yerian, M.A.
Margaret A. Yerian, M.A.

Art Director
Thomas Petiet, M.F.A.

Designer
Cameron John Yerian

Senior Editor
Mary Rush, M.F.A.
Sharon Irvine, B.A.

Contributors
Nancy Muhlbach, M.A.
Jerry Gillmore, B.A.
Mary White, B.A.
Edith Wolter, B.S.
Susan Keezer
Virginia Foster, A.B.

Editorial Assistant
Phoebe A. Yerian

Readability Consultants
Donald E.P. Smith, Ph.D.
School of Education
University of Michigan

Judith K. Smith, Ph.D.
University of Michigan

Instructional Development Consultant
Joel B. Fleming, M.A.
Instructional Development & Technology
Michigan State University

Synectics Consultant
Gershom Clark Morningstar, M.A.
President, Wolverine-Morningstar Media

Library Consultant
Noel Winkler, M.A.L.S.
Lecturer, Children's Literature
Elementary Librarian, Media Center
School of Education
University of Michigan

Library of Congress Cataloging in Publication Data
Main entry under title:

Weird gardens.

(Fun time activities)
Includes index.
SUMMARY: Step-by-step directions for a number
of experiments and projects involving plants, such
as exploring good and bad microbes, sprouting seeds,
and growing and training a variety of plants.
1. Gardening—Juvenile literature. 2. Botany—
Experiments—Juvenile literature. 3. Plant
propagation—Juvenile literature. |1. Botany—
Experiments. 2. Gardening] I. Yerian, Cameron John.
II. Yerian, Margaret.
SB457.W45   581'.028   75-15601
ISBN 0-516-01322-X

Contents

INVISIBLE SEEDS

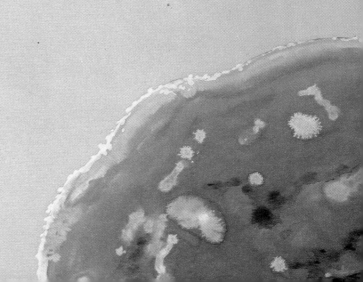

Hidden Seeds

PRETEND you are a kitchen scientist. You are going to grow some very strange plants.

GROW some invisible seeds. They are called microbes. They don't carry their lunch with them as real seeds do. You have to feed them to make them grow.

FIND OUT where the seeds are hiding. They are so small you can't see them. But they are around you all the time.

SET OUT some food for the microbes. Use a chunk of banana, a piece of cooked potato, and a little fruit juice.

PUT the banana and potato on a piece of aluminum foil. Pour an inch or two of juice in a glass.

LEAVE the food in the air for 1/2 hour. The microbes will plant themselves.

COVER the potato and banana with a bowl. Put some kind of lid on the glass.

SET the food in a warm, dark place.

WAIT 2 or 3 days. Then go back and look at the food. How many kinds of hidden seeds fell from the air? Each kind will look a little different.

GET a magnifying glass and look closely at what you grew. Does it scare you? Just scare it back.

7

Strange Gardening

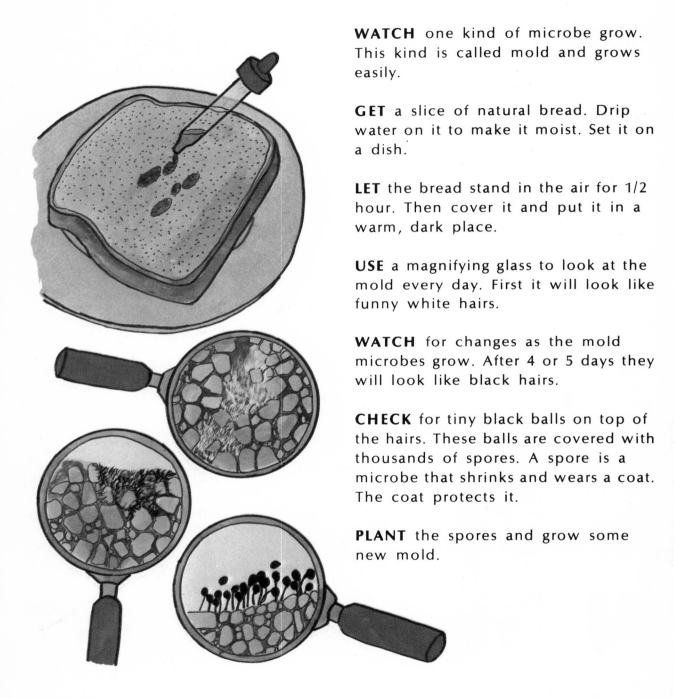

WATCH one kind of microbe grow. This kind is called mold and grows easily.

GET a slice of natural bread. Drip water on it to make it moist. Set it on a dish.

LET the bread stand in the air for 1/2 hour. Then cover it and put it in a warm, dark place.

USE a magnifying glass to look at the mold every day. First it will look like funny white hairs.

WATCH for changes as the mold microbes grow. After 4 or 5 days they will look like black hairs.

CHECK for tiny black balls on top of the hairs. These balls are covered with thousands of spores. A spore is a microbe that shrinks and wears a coat. The coat protects it.

PLANT the spores and grow some new mold.

GET another piece of moist bread. Put it on a dish as before.

TOUCH the spores on your mold garden with a toothpick. Be very gentle.

TAP the center of the new bread with the toothpick. Cover it and wait a day.

LOOK at the second piece of bread with the magnifying glass. You can't see a spore. But you can see where you planted it.

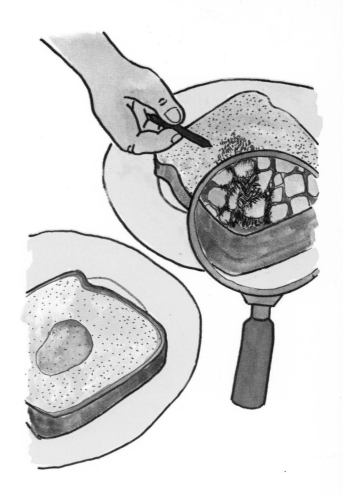

MAKE another kind of garden from mold microbes. Use an old orange or lemon. Cut it in half.

LEAVE the fruit in the air. Then cover it and wait a few days for the mold to grow. Check the spore balls with the magnifying glass.

LOOK for little branches that hold the spores. You can move these spores to a new home too. Grow it as you did the bread mold.

You can become the gardener in a very strange garden.

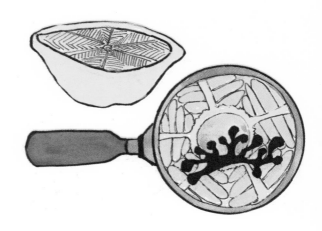

Zonking the Microbes

FIND OUT how to control microbes. You have to live with them. But you can make them do what you want most of the time.

CHECK on what temperature does to microbes.

WAIT until the next time your mother uses frozen vegetables. Ask her to save a few for you.

DIVIDE the vegetables up in 3 small dishes. Leave all of them in the air for 1/2 hour.

COVER the dishes and put one back in the freezer. Set another in the refrigerator.

LEAVE the third dish in a warm, moist place. Check each dish after a few days. Which one did the microbes attack first?

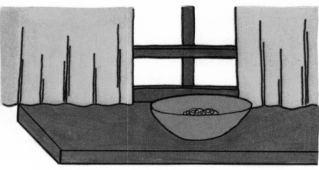

SEE what else a microbe needs to live. Get some grapes. Put them in two different dishes.

LEAVE one dish in the house. Put the other out in the hot sun. The ones in the sun will wrinkle and look like raisins. What happens to the grapes you left in the house?

SOAK the dried up grapes in water. Now leave them in the house. Do microbes grow now?

TRY another experiment with moisture.

GET a few dried beans like navy beans or dried limas. Get 2 glasses. Put a few beans in each glass. Cover the beans in one glass with water.

FIND 2 more glasses and some flour. Put 1 tablespoon of flour in each glass.

ADD water to one glass. Now wait a few days. Where are the microbes?

Think of other ways people keep microbes from growing.

Pushing the Microbes

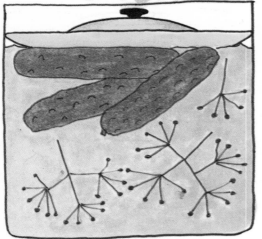

HELP the microbes do good things. Not all of these invisible seeds turn food into something that looks like it should go in the garbage.

GIVE some microbes a cucumber to work on. Make them help you. You'll probably end up with a pickle.

PUT 1/4 cup of salt in a quart container. Fill it with water.

GET a quart jar. Put a few cloves of garlic and some fresh dill in it. Add 1 tablespoon of pickling spices. You can get these at a grocery store if you need to buy them.

DROP 3 or 4 small cucumbers into the jar. Then pour in the salt water from the first container. Cover the jar with a lid.

LEAVE the jar in a cool place. After a day, go back and look at the cucumbers. The microbes got busy right away, didn't they?

WATCH your cucumbers for the next 2 weeks. Check for differences in the size. See if the cucumbers stay in the top of the jar where you put them.

LOOK for changes caused by the growing microbes. They will make the water go out of the cucumbers. The color will change as the water leaves.

SCRAPE OFF any scum that comes to the top. You might have to do this quite a few times. Yeast microbes like to grow on cucumbers too.

TAKE a cucumber out of the jar after a week. Cut it in half to see how well the microbes are doing their job.

CUT another cucumber after 2 weeks. Those busy microbes have changed it again. It's a pickle now.

GO AHEAD and have a taste.

Mystic Microbes

FIND OUT what else microbes do for you every day. Give them your help and have some fun.

LET the microbes go to work on a dish of milk. Set the milk in the air and watch it carefully.

WAIT until the milk turns sour and forms curds. Right after this happens, get a piece of cheesecloth or a fine strainer. Strain the curds.

ADD some salt to the curds that are left in the strainer. You just helped the microbes make cottage cheese.

FIND another good use for growing microbes.

GET two bowls that are the same size. Put 1/2 cup of flour, 1 tablespoon of sugar, and 3 tablespoons of water in each one.

STIR the mixtures. Keep one bowl in the air. Put the other in the refrigerator.

LET the mixtures stand overnight.

TAKE the bowl from the refrigerator. Set it next to the one left in the air. What happened to the outside dough?

LOOK at both bowls carefully. Yeast microbes fell from the air. They planted themselves in the outside bowl and grew. Then they made a special kind of air that puffed up the dough.

SPEED UP the puffing by using yeast that comes in a package. Big companies grow yeast plants for people. Then bread can be made without waiting for the yeast microbes to plant themselves.

MAKE one mixture exactly as before. Change the other one a little.

USE the same amounts of flour and sugar. But add 1 teaspoon of yeast to the 3 tablespoons of water. This is about 1 million microbes.

MAKE SURE the water is just warm. Yeast plants will not grow in cold water. Hot water will kill them.

ADD the yeast mixture to the flour and sugar. Stir it all together.

LEAVE both bowls in the air for 2 or 3 hours. Then see how much faster it is to do the planting for the microbes.

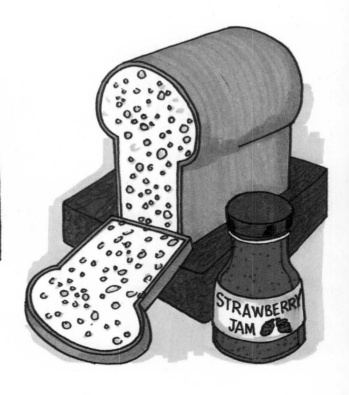

THINK how great it must have been when people found out about yeast. It got rid of tough bread and sore jaws.

Microbes Help a Rot

FILL a container with soil. Put 3 or 4 grapes on it. Sprinkle a small handful of soil over the fruit. Water it.

SET the container outside where it won't get spilled. Watch the grapes change.

WAIT 4 or 5 weeks. Then dig up some of the top soil. The grapes nearly disappeared didn't they? The microbes did it again.

LOOK for other places where the microbes worked this way. Dig down in a pile of rotting leaves or grass.

LOOK for molds and yeasts growing on the dead material. These microbes will do their work until the pile is gone.

MAKE food for plants this way. The soil that is left will have invisible food in it. Plants need this special food to grow.

MIX this rich soil with other soil before you use it. You won't want your plants to overeat.

Root of the Matter

Think about how special microbes are. Each kind of microbe is different. Each grows only in a certain material.

Look around you. Millions of microbes are floating in the air all the time. You can see what they do. But you can't see them or feel them.

Sometimes these invisible seeds grow where you don't want them. What they grow is very interesting. But you end up with something for the garbage can.

Plant the microbes where you want them. They can turn one kind of food into another. You can have fluffy bread instead of flat bread. You can have pickles instead of cucumbers.

Think about what microbes do for all living things. The soil has plant food because of microbes. Animals eat because of the plants. People eat because of the plants and animals.

Each growing part helps another growing part. And it all starts with the microbes.

MINOR
MIRACLES

Bean Burst-Out

ASK your mother for two empty pill bottles. Use the plastic kind with snap-on caps.

GET some bean seeds. Fill one bottle with seeds. Mark it.

FILL the other bottle with bean seeds and water. Mark this one in a different way.

PUT the caps on the bottles. Make sure they are on tight.

CHECK the bottles for the next few days. It's a little like tight clothes when you eat too much isn't it?

Small World Window

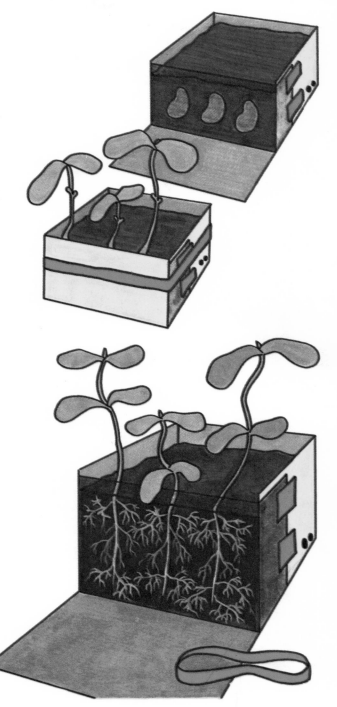

GET a milk carton. Cut off the top to make it a square box.

PUNCH some holes in the sides of the box. Put them near the bottom.

CUT 2 corners down as far as the bottom of the box. Leave it hooked at the bottom. This is the window.

LAY the window flat. Pull a piece of plastic wrap tightly across the opening. Tape it to the standing sides of the box.

CLOSE the window. Put a rubber band around the whole carton to keep the window shut.

FILL the box almost to the top with soil. Put 3 or 4 bean or pea seeds in it. Lay them next to the plastic wrap.

COVER the seeds with a small handful of soil. Keep it moist all the time.

OPEN the window of your small world to watch the seeds germinate and grow. From beginning to end you are there.

Teeny Tester

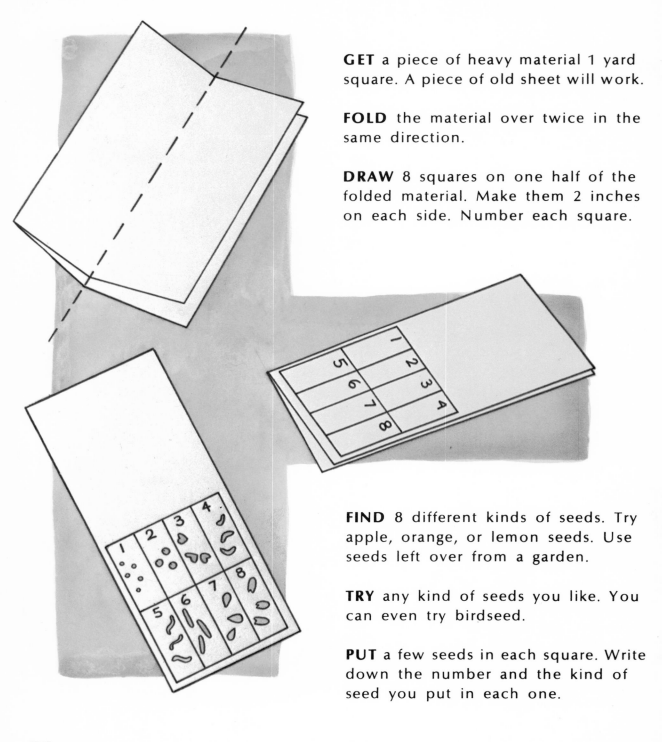

GET a piece of heavy material 1 yard square. A piece of old sheet will work.

FOLD the material over twice in the same direction.

DRAW 8 squares on one half of the folded material. Make them 2 inches on each side. Number each square.

FIND 8 different kinds of seeds. Try apple, orange, or lemon seeds. Use seeds left over from a garden.

TRY any kind of seeds you like. You can even try birdseed.

PUT a few seeds in each square. Write down the number and the kind of seed you put in each one.

FOLD the other half of the material over the seeds. Roll up the tester.

TIE a piece of string 3 inches from each end. Keep the strings loose.

WET the tester until it drips. Keep it in a warm, moist place for a week.

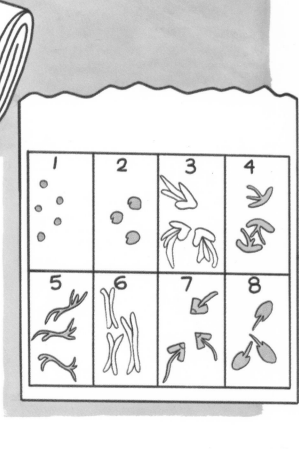

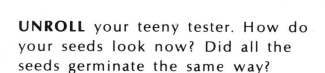

UNROLL your teeny tester. How do your seeds look now? Did all the seeds germinate the same way?

TRY the experiment again with weed seeds. Use milk pod, sunflower, or burdock seeds.

USE whatever grows near your home. A weed is only a plant growing in the wrong place anyway.

Egg Carton Botany

GET a styrofoam egg carton. Punch a small hole in the bottom of each cup.

FILL the cups with soil. Drop 2 bean seeds in each. Cover them with about as much soil as the size of the seed.

PUT your egg carton garden in a moist, warm place. Give the seeds a drink of water when the soil looks thirsty.

WAIT until the seedlings come through the soil and are about 2 inches high. Then cut the egg carton apart between the cups. Now begin experimenting.

DIVIDE the cups into sets of two. Give each set a number so you can remember what you did with each one. Make a list of what you do.

EXPERIMENT with light on one set. Keep one cup in a light, happy place. Put the other in a dark place.

USE one set to check on heat. Let one cup of seedlings live in a warm place. Give the other a cold home.

LET one set tell you about water. Treat one cup to a drink of water when it looks dry. Let the other go thirsty.

SEE what air does with the fourth set. Put a jar upside down over one cup. Leave its friend in the open air.

FIND OUT about a seedling's lunch. Pull off the fleshy, winglike part from one cup in the fifth set. This is a cotyledon. Let the other cup keep its wings.

TAKE OFF the middle leaves of one seedling in the last set. Leave the other cup alone.

WAIT about a week. Check every day to see how your seedlings are growing. Did all of them get what they needed to live?

Simple Celery

GET a stalk of celery. Find a large one with leaves.

CUT a little of the stalk off at the bottom to make the end flat. Then make a 3 inch cut up the middle.

GET two small dishes. Cover the bottom of each with water.

ADD 25 drops of food coloring to the water in each dish. Use two different colors.

PUT one end of the celery in each dish. Lean the top of the stalk up against something.

WAIT an hour. Then go back and look at the celery. Leave it in the water overnight. Then look at it again. You will be able to see how leaves feed a plant.

FIND the veins in the leaves. They are the food carriers. Did you know you were built a little like a stalk of celery?

Lawn on a Sponge

GET a new sponge and wet it. Put it on a shallow dish.

SPRINKLE a handful of grass seed on the sponge. Put it on thick. Have the same amount all over.

GIVE your grass seed some water every day.

POUR the water on gently to keep the seeds from piling on top of each other. Better yet, fill an old window cleaner bottle with water. Spray it on.

USE a natural sponge or a man-made sponge.

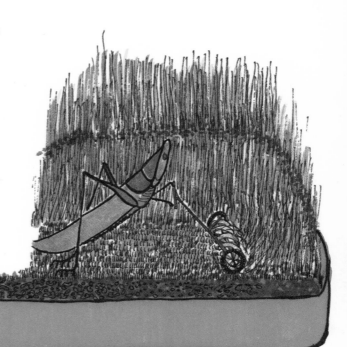

SET your private lawn where it will get some sunlight every day. Check it with a magnifying glass if you like.

LOOK for the path of the roots. They will find space to grow.

WATCH your grass grow. Now you have your own lawn. And you won't even have to mow it.

Sprouting Ideas

GROW an indoor feast without soil. You don't even need a green thumb! Begin by washing a quart jar thoroughly.

MEASURE OUT a tablespoonful of seed. Try alfalfa seeds or mung beans. Wash the seeds well. Put them in the jar with 4 tablespoonsful of lukewarm water. Let them soak overnight.

FIND a ring to fit the jar. Cut a piece of screen or two layers of cheesecloth to fit inside of the ring.

PUT this top on the jar the next morning and pour off the water. Save it! Use the vitamin-filled water to cook with.

RINSE the seeds with fresh lukewarm water. Drain it off. Put the jar on its side under the kitchen sink.

SHAKE the tiny sprouts gently whenever you rinse them. This keeps them from growing together in one thick mat.

GIVE them this bath two or three times a day. They love it. Always drain off the water and return the jar to its hideout.

WATCH for white, hairy roots to creep out. It will take a day or two.

EAT the bean sprouts when they are 2 to 4 inches long and haven't yet grown leaves. Keep them in a covered jar of water in the refrigerator. Change the water every day. They keep almost a week.

GROW the alfalfa sprouts until they form tiny leaves. Bring them out into the sunlight for a few hours. Watch them turn green. When they turn green, they are ready to eat.

RINSE all sprouts well before you eat them. Drop the alfalfa sprouts into a bag with a few paper towels.

SHAKE the bag GENTLY. Don't bruise the tender sprouts. When they are fluffy, pop them into a container with a tight lid. Keep them in the refrigerator.

TRY sprouting lentils, winter wheat, water cress, or any grain or seed you could ordinarily eat. You will be sprouting new ideas every day.

Root of the Matter

Think about all the different kinds of seeds there are. They can be any size. They can be any shape. Seeds can be bumpy or smooth. They come in almost any color. No matter how they look, they all grow into something wonderful.

All seeds carry their lunch with them. The baby plant snuggles between the cotyledons. They feed the baby until it can eat by itself. Then the roots get busy and pull the food from the soil. The leaves know it's time to begin their job. They hold food and send it to the plant.

Some seeds need a lot of help and are hard to grow. Some nearly grow by themselves. No matter what kind of help they need, each plant is special. Each kind of seed turns into a different plant. And each plant has a different leaf. The best way to repay nature is to take care of one of her plants.

The Eyes Have It

FIND a firm potato with beautiful eyes. Beautiful eyes in a potato are sort of green and full of life.

CUT the potato into pieces. There must be at least one eye in each piece. This is the growth bud. Let the pieces dry for a day.

PLANT each piece about 4 inches deep in well-worked soil.

PILE soil up around the plants when they are about 5 inches tall.

FEEL down into the soil carefully after the plant gets big. Tiny potatoes will be forming. These are called tubers. Soon they will be big enough to dig up and eat.

TRY GROWING a potato plant in a plastic garbage bag 1/2 full of soil. You won't believe it. Those beautiful "eyes" did it again!

Turning on the Bulbs

BUY a sleeping hyacinth or tulip bulb in early summer. Maybe a friend or neighbor has an extra one to give you.

TURN it upside down. With a paring knife, make a cut about 1/3 of the way into the bottom of the bulb. Make two more cuts the same way. They should criss-cross in the middle.

PUT the bulb upside down in a box or paper bag. Keep it at regular house temperature (70 to 80 degrees) through the summer. Leave it alone.

PEEK inside after two or three months. You'll be amazed at all the little bulblets that formed. Where did they come from?

PLANT the bountiful bulb outside in the fall. Be sure to keep it in the same upside-down position. Cover it with about 3 inches of soil.

Can you imagine what will happen in the spring?!

PLANT PUZZLE

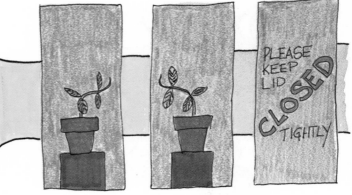

PLEASE KEEP LID CLOSED TIGHTLY

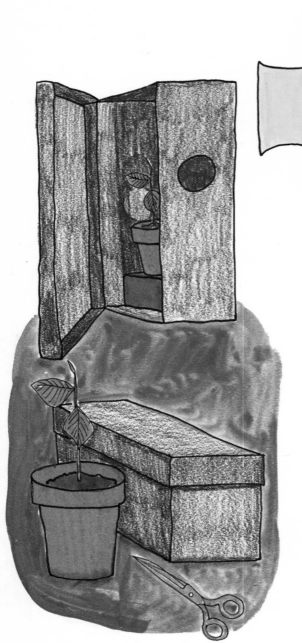

PLANT a bean or pea seed in a small pot. Wait until it is about 4 inches high and growing well. Then find a large shoe box.

CUT a hole in the side of the box. Put it in the middle. Stand the box on end.

SET the pot on a smaller box. Put the small box and plant inside the shoe box.

PUT the lid on the shoe box. Place it where a lot of light will shine on the hole.

OPEN the box every day. Give the plant some water and see how far it's grown toward the hole.

34

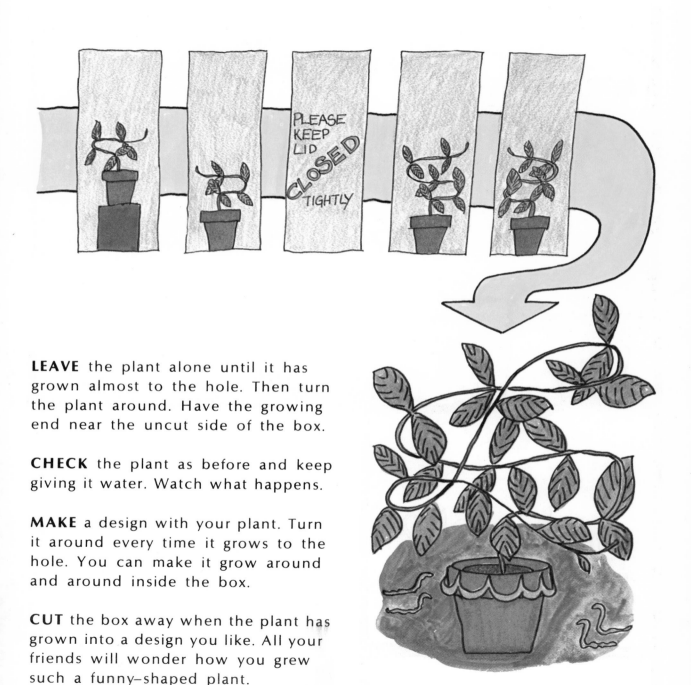

LEAVE the plant alone until it has grown almost to the hole. Then turn the plant around. Have the growing end near the uncut side of the box.

CHECK the plant as before and keep giving it water. Watch what happens.

MAKE a design with your plant. Turn it around every time it grows to the hole. You can make it grow around and around inside the box.

CUT the box away when the plant has grown into a design you like. All your friends will wonder how you grew such a funny-shaped plant.

35

Crazy Climbers

PREPARE two pots for planting. In one plant a few morning glory seeds. Plant wisteria seeds in the other.

SLIP each pot into a clear plastic bag. Fasten it loosely at the top.

REMOVE the bag once the vines poke their heads up.

WATCH them grow. After a few days they will be falling all over themselves.

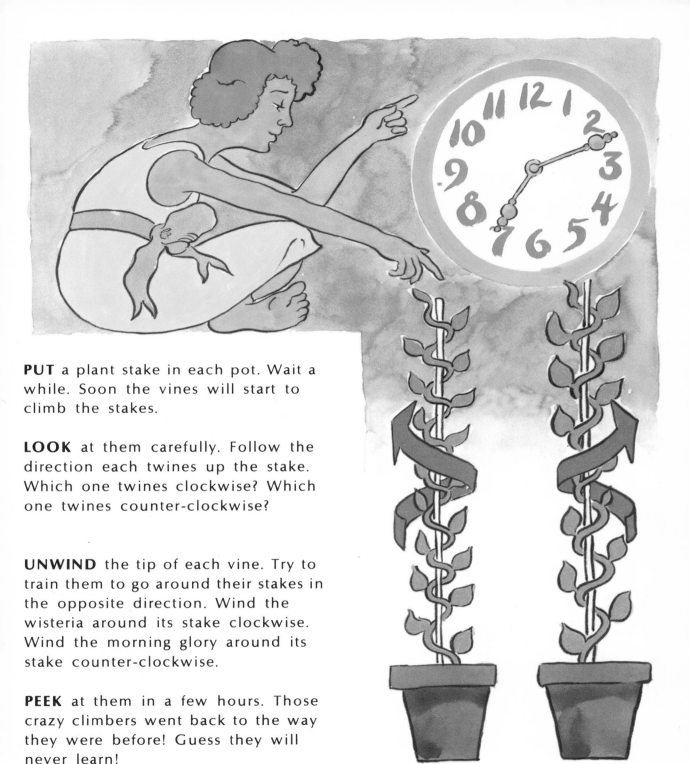

PUT a plant stake in each pot. Wait a while. Soon the vines will start to climb the stakes.

LOOK at them carefully. Follow the direction each twines up the stake. Which one twines clockwise? Which one twines counter-clockwise?

UNWIND the tip of each vine. Try to train them to go around their stakes in the opposite direction. Wind the wisteria around its stake clockwise. Wind the morning glory around its stake counter-clockwise.

PEEK at them in a few hours. Those crazy climbers went back to the way they were before! Guess they will never learn!

37

Ups & Downs

GROW a coleus plant 8 or 10 inches tall. The straighter it is the better.

LAY the potted coleus on its side. Make sure it is in a sunny spot.

WAIT a day or two. Look at the plant. What is it trying to do? The top of the plant is trying to bend upward toward the light. The top wants to be up even though the pot is lying down.

LOOSEN the soil in the pot. Take hold of the base of the plant. Gently pull the rooted soil from the pot. Study the roots. What are they trying to do? They are bending down toward the under side of the pot. Gravity tells them that the ground should be below them and not out the end of a sideways pot.

PUT the plant roots back in the pot. Be careful to press down the soil around them. Give it a little drink. Now try to train it the opposite way. It takes a while.

Can you ever get it straight again?

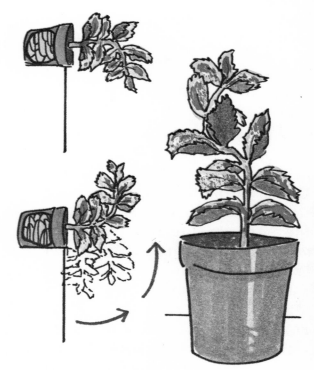

No Pokes for Plants

FIND OUT how careful plant roots are. Get 3 large bean seeds. Push the sharp end of a needle into each one.

STICK the other end of the needles into a big cork. Set the cork on a plate filled with water.

COVER the cork and seeds with a clear glass. Put the glass upside down. Make sure it doesn't touch the seeds.

WAIT for the seeds to germinate and start growing roots. Watch for the roots to grow down.

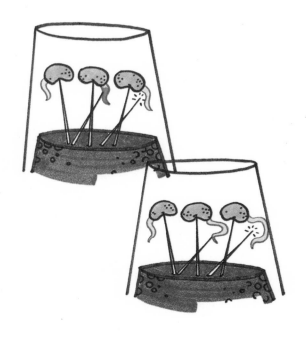

GET 2 more needles when the roots are hanging down. Push the dull end of one needle into the cork. Fasten it so it is in the path of the growing root.

PUSH the point of the other needle into another root. Do it near the tip.

WATCH what happens to these roots. See how you changed their growth? Just like you, they stay away from things that hurt them.

Turn Signals

GIVE a new direction to your plants. You can make them grow short, tall, fat or skinny.

USE two small geranium plants about 6 inches tall for this training session.

TRIM all of the side leaves on one. Leave only the top few groups of leaves. Keep the plant trimmed this way as it grows.

FASTEN it loosely to a plant stake when it gets too tall to stand up on its own. Soon it will look something like a lollipop.

PINCH OFF the newest top leaves of the second plant. Use your fingernails or a pair of scissors.

WATCH what happens. Two new growing tips will start to reach out. Let them grow a while.

PINCH OFF the newest leaves on these two tips. Each of these will then form two more new tips. Now there are four. Pinch those and you will have eight branches. Where will it end?

COMPARE the two plants after several weeks. Did they follow your turn signals?

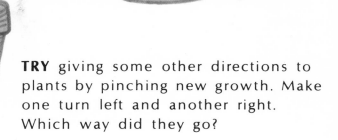

TRY giving some other directions to plants by pinching new growth. Make one turn left and another right. Which way did they go?

41

Beginners' Bonsai

LOOK around your yard for tree seedlings that have sprouted on their own. Maple, willow, pine, spruce, or juniper would work. Pick out one that is 6 to 10 inches tall. Don't dig it up yet! Buy a plant at the nursery if you can't find one in your yard.

GET a container that is almost as wide as your tree is tall. It must be shallow, only 3 to 5 inches deep. A beautiful container is very important for Bonsai plantings.

CUT OFF the bottom of a clean plastic gallon jug if you don't have another container. (It's better than nothing!)

MAKE SURE there are drainage holes in the container. Cover them with broken pot pieces or screen. Spread a thin layer of gravel over the bottom. Add an inch of your potting soil mix. For evergreens use half soil and half sand or perlite.

SIFT soil over the roots with a sieve or piece of screen. When the roots are covered, press the soil down gently around them. There can't be air pockets around the roots.

SPRINKLE water on your Bonsai until it runs out the drainage holes. Sprinkle it only lightly as needed after that.

KEEP it out of sun and wind until it gets strong.

TRAIN your tree to look old. Wind covered 20 gauge wire around the trunk while it is young and easily bent. Shape it carefully. Let the wire stay on for several weeks until the tree gets the right idea.

TELL your Bonsai how to grow by cutting off twigs that head in the wrong direction.

READ about Bonsai. Learn about Bonsai. Grow with your Bonsai. With proper care it will give you a lifetime of enjoyment. Maybe two lifetimes!

Root of the Matter

Plants are living things. Much like you, they need light, air, food, and water to live. Also like you, they need love and care.

Plants have feelings. They avoid things that might hurt them. They grow toward things they need or like. They don't like to be too hot or too cold, too wet or too dry. Look for their signals. They will tell you lots of things.

Give them a comfortable pot, an occasional bath, and the right growing conditions. They will grow happy, healthy, and beautiful.

Discover the many tricks your plant can do. Try to teach them others. Train a vine to crawl through a hole, circle a window, or peek over a fence.

Get friends to try training plants too. Share your training secrets.

Learn about the laws of nature that make each trick possible. Knowing these, you'll think up a bunch of new tricks, without a doubt.

INDEX

ILLUSTRATORS

About the Editors

Cameron John and Margaret A. Yerian have advanced degrees in psychology and mass communications from the University of Michigan. They have been active in educational and instructional writing for both adults and children, with many publications to their credit. Their work has ranged from the Educational Television Project in American Samoa, where Mrs. Yerian served as a producer/director and Mr. Yerian was a writer and editor to their present work as media consultants in the Detroit metropolitan area.